DIVINE TRANSPLANT

UPROOTED FOR GROWTH

OSHANE HINES

Hines Press

Edited by Hines Press

Book cover generated by Author using Midjourney AI V5.2 2023

Published by Hines Press

Casper, WY

ISBN: 978-1-7376173-5-8 (Ebook)

ISBN: 978-1-7376173-6-5(Paperback)

LCCN : 2023912621

INTRODUCTION

Each journey begins with a single step. For a seed, this first step is buried in the dark soil. Although silent, humble, and seemingly insignificant, the seed houses a world of potential that mirrors the divine purpose in each of us. The soil, with its inherent limitations and constraints, stands as a metaphor for our own lives. We often find ourselves feeling restrained, confined to a small space, and yearning for something more. However, it is within this very soil that we discover the essential nourishment required for our growth.

During the initial stages of growth. The seed confronts the harsh realities of its environment. The growth process becomes an embodiment of struggles, adversities, and eventual breakthroughs. Similarly, as humans, we grapple with an array of challenges. In these moments, we might not grasp the extent to which our resilience is being developed. However, these trials are critical, sculpting the strength and determination necessary for survival and prosperity.

Each seed is reliant on key nutrients for growth: water, sunlight, and minerals drawn from the soil. A similar analogy can be drawn to our spiritual lives. Prayer, faith, and love act as the spiritual sustenance that fosters our growth. These elements empower us, enabling us to push through the soil of adversity, reaching for the sunlight of achievement.

Pruning is an essential phase of a plant's life cycle that promotes healthier, more vigorous growth. It involves eliminating parts of the plant that may seem healthy but are, in actuality, impeding its overall growth. In a similar vein, God often removes things to which we are attached, creating room for us to grow stronger and better. Although this can be a painful process, it is one that yields a richer, more abundant harvest.

The notion of a divine transplant marks a pivotal transition. God, acting as the divine gardener, relocates us from a familiar setting to an unfamiliar one. Though initially intimidating, this transplant forms an integral part of our growth. In this new environment, we encounter fresh challenges and experiences that serve to foster our development.

Divine Transplant: "Uprooted for Growth" welcomes you to embark on an enlightening journey. This book explores the profound connections between our spiritual evolution and the intricacies of the natural world. Through the analogy of agricultural growth, it provides a distinct perspective on the stages of spiritual development. Each chapter is crafted to navigate readers through their unique divine transplant, shedding light on the enriching journey and the plentiful spiritual harvest that lies ahead.

SEED IN THE SOIL

he journey begins, much like the life of a seed. This is not a tale of rapid success or instant maturity, but a narrative of slow, sometimes painful growth. Of lessons learned in the darkness, where roots anchor deep in the soil, seeking life-sustaining nutrients and water. A seed sprouts under the earth, out of sight, preparing to emerge into the world.

Seeds may seem simple, small, and unremarkable, yet within each one lies the potential for greatness. A tiny acorn holds the blueprint for a towering oak tree, just as the potential for personal growth and divine purpose resides within every person. The journey starts with understanding and accepting humble beginnings. A seed, despite its size and seeming insignificance, carries vast potential. Similarly, people, regardless of where they come from or their current circumstances, possess an innate capacity for growth and development.

Every seed begins its journey in the soil — dark, dense, and possibly stifling. This beginning may seem restrictive, but the soil is not a prison; it is a cradle of life. It nourishes the seed, providing it with vital nutrients, and a safe environment to grow and establish roots. Our circumstances, no matter how challenging, serve a similar purpose. They nourish our spirit, strengthen our character, and teach us valuable lessons about perseverance, resilience, and faith.

Seeds do not grow in perfect conditions. They face challenges such as insufficient water or nutrients, pests, and harsh weather. But these adversities do not halt their growth. On the contrary, they stimulate it. The struggle to reach for water and nutrients deepens their roots, making them more resilient to future trials. Similarly, we face numerous adversities. Problems can be likened to the harsh conditions a seed faces. They stimulate our personal and spiritual growth, deepening our roots and making us more resilient and better equipped to face future trials.

It is easy to underestimate a seed. They are small, inconspicuous, often buried, and forgotten. But within every seed lies a promise, a potential for life that waits to be nurtured and cultivated. No matter how insignificant we may feel, we must never forget that we have a purpose, a potential that God wishes to cultivate.

Seeds require patience. They do not grow overnight. It takes time for a seed to break through the shell, develop roots, and sprout through the soil. We must learn from the seed. The journey of growth is not a sprint, but a marathon. It's about consistency, about taking small steps toward growth every day. It's about learning to be patient with ourselves, and understanding that meaningful growth takes time.

In the seed's journey, we find parallels in our lives. It begins in the soil, in darkness, but with every day, it moves closer to the light. It grows stronger, more resilient, and ready to face the world. And when it finally breaks through the soil, it is not the end of its journey, but the beginning. It becomes a symbol of hope, a testament to the power of perseverance.

The seed's journey is our journey. We begin in our soil, with our limitations and challenges. But these do not define us. They are the starting point, the catalyst for our growth. And just like the seed, we have the potential to grow, to rise above our circumstances, to bloom where we are planted, and eventually, to be ready for our divine transplant.

Each of us is a seed. We carry within us the potential for greatness. Our humble beginnings, our struggles, our experiences — they are the soil that nourishes us, the foundation upon which we grow. The seed in the soil is the start of the journey.

Reflecting on my own beginnings, I was born and raised in a small town named Grange Hill in Westmoreland, Jamaica. Life there was akin to a seed nestled in rocky soil. My hometown was infamous for community violence and several devastating massacres rather than its picturesque landscapes or welcoming communities. Amidst conflict and scarcity, where resources were as elusive as moments of peace, the seed of my life was planted.

My childhood was divided between my parents. I spent my early years with my father until he passed away untimely from diabetes when I was just 10 years of age. Following that, I moved in with my mother, marking the beginning of a new chapter in my life. Despite the hardships, I began to recognize these scarce resources and struggles as my own soil—my foundation for growth.

Our home was modest, a one-bedroom board house with external facilities. There were five of us—my mother, step-dad, brother, and I. We made the most of our small space. My stepdad, the sole breadwinner of our family, labored tirelessly at a sugar factory, riding his bicycle to work each day. His earnings, though meager, kept our family afloat.

Despite our economic struggles, my mother was unyielding in her dedication to our education. She was a beacon of resilience and determination, instilling in my brother and I the belief in education as a pathway to transcend our circumstances. Even though she hadn't completed school herself, she was adamant that we would not follow the same path. We were enrolled in the government assistance program for food at school, and while we walked to middle school each day, through high school we only had enough funds for transportation.

In 2014, I graduated from the prestigious Manning's School, a renowned traditional high school in my community. With six Caribbean secondary (CXC) subjects under my belt, I became the first-generation student in my family. This achievement was a testament to my mother's unwavering faith in education and her sacrifices.

This was my seed's journey—marked by humble beginnings, challenges, and personal growth. It was the soil that nourished my spirit, deepened my roots, and shaped my character. This journey prepared me for the divine transplant that was yet to come.

2

GROWING PAINS

*E*very seed experiences a time of growth, and it is during this time that it faces the most challenges. Breaking through the hard shell, pushing through the soil, reaching for the sun, all while establishing roots. Growth is a demanding process, involving a lot of struggle and discomfort. Yet, it is this process that transforms the seed into a plant. The struggles and discomforts a seed experiences during growth can be likened to the growing pains we experience in life.

Growing pains are a part of the growth process. They are the struggles, trials, and tribulations we face on our journey of growth and self-discovery. They can come in many forms - such as loss, adversity, hardship, or failure. But each growing pain, each struggle, is an opportunity for us to grow and evolve.

Reflecting on my journey, the growing pains become evident. The loss of my father at a young age was a significant growing pain. It was a deep wound, one that took time to heal. Yet, it was through this loss that I learned about the impermanence of life, about grief, and about resilience. It was a challenging time, but it was also a time of immense personal growth.

Living in a single room with my mother, stepfather, and brother was another growing pain. The space was cramped, the resources scarce. There was very little privacy and very little space to call my own. But it was in this small space that I learned about love, sacrifice, and about the importance of family. I saw firsthand the sacrifices my parents made for our family and the lengths they would go to ensure that we had a better future. This experience was a catalyst for my personal growth.

Walking to school every day was a physical reminder of our financial constraints. It was a daily struggle, one that required determination and resilience. But it was also a growing pain, one that taught me the value of perseverance, the importance of education, and the lengths one needs to go to attain it. This struggle became a stepping stone on my journey of growth.

The hostile community in Grange Hill, known more for its violence and massacres than its sense of community, was a painful reality to grow up in. Yet, even within this harsh environment, I learned about resilience, about survival, and about the strength of the human spirit. I saw how, despite the adversities, life moved on, people adapted and found ways to survive. This experience instilled in me a strong survival instinct, a drive to overcome adversity, and a desire to create a better future for myself and those around me.

My stepfather's daily labor at the sugar factory and his dedicated commute by bicycle was vivid lesson in hard work and determination. Despite the grueling work and minimal pay, he never faltered, instilling in me a strong work ethic and the realization that perseverance can pave the way to greater opportunities.

My mother's dedication to our education, despite her

own lack of formal education, taught me about sacrifice, about putting others before oneself. It was through her sacrifices that I was able to graduate from a reputable high school and become a first-generation student. Her belief in the power of education became the foundation for my own belief in self-improvement and personal growth.

Like the seed that struggles to push through the soil and reach for the sun, we too experience struggles and discomforts as we grow. But these growing pains are necessary for our transformation. They shape us, mold us, and prepare us for the journey ahead. They make us stronger, more resilient, and more prepared for the divine transplant that awaits us.

Each growing pain, each struggle, is a testament to our strength and resilience. They are reminders of our journey, of how far we have come, and of how much more we are capable of achieving. These struggles are not meant to break us, but to build us, to shape us into the individuals we are destined to become.

The difficulties faced while living in a one-bedroom home did not confine me; they expanded my understanding of sacrifice, love, and the resilience of the human spirit. This humble space became a school, teaching me lessons that no formal education could.

Walking to school each day, a journey that highlighted our financial struggles wasn't just a physical commute. It was a testament to the importance of education and the lengths we would go to acquire it. The journey was not easy, but the knowledge and opportunities it led to make every step worth it.

Growing up in the volatile environment of Grange Hill was undoubtedly a challenge. But it was also a teacher, an instructor of survival, resilience, and the will to aspire for a better future. It taught me to find strength in adversity, to adapt, and persevere.

Watching my stepfather pedal to the sugar factory daily was more than a memory. It was a living lesson in dedication, perseverance, and the relentless pursuit of providing for one's family. It was a testament to the power of hard work, and it ingrained in me an unyielding work ethic.

Experiencing my mother's unwavering commitment to our education, despite her own lack of formal education, was a powerful lesson in sacrifice, resilience, and the transformative power of knowledge. It was through her faith in the power of education that I became a first-generation student, breaking barriers and setting a new course for my family.

Each of these experiences, these growing pains, have shaped my journey, preparing me for the divine transplant. Like the seed, I have been nourished by the soil of my circumstances, grown through the struggles, and prepared for my future transformation.

Remember, no seed grows without experiencing the hardships of breaking through its shell, pushing through the soil, and reaching for the sun. Similarly, no person grows without experiencing growing pains. They are an integral part of our journey, the catalysts of our growth and transformation. As we move forward, let us remember that our growing pains are not roadblocks, but stepping stones leading to our divine transplant.

3

THE POWER OF NUTRIENTS

*E*very seed requires nutrients to grow. It needs nitrogen to build strong roots, phosphorus for energy transfer, and potassium for water regulation. Micro elements such as iron, zinc, copper, and molybdenum are also essential as they participate in various life processes. These nutrients, sourced from the soil, enable the seed to sprout, reach toward the light, and blossom into a plant.

In parallel, our spiritual growth depends on certain nutrients. However, these nutrients aren't found in the soil but in our life experiences, the people we encounter, and the challenges we conquer. They nourish our souls, fuel our growth, and aid us in becoming the individuals we are destined to be.

Faith acts as our nitrogen, forming the foundation of our spiritual lives. It helps us establish deep roots in our beliefs and gives us the strength to stand firm in the face of adversity. Faith doesn't make things easy; it makes them possible. It reassures us that we are not alone in our journey and that there is a divine power guiding us, shaping us, and preparing us for our future.

Hope is our phosphorus, the energy that propels us

forward. It fuels our dreams, gives us the strength to over-come obstacles, and keeps us moving forward. When times are tough, when our journey becomes challenging, hope illuminates our path, reminding us that better days lie ahead. It is the light that shines in the darkness, guiding us toward our divine transplant.

Love is our potassium, controlling the flow of kindness and compassion in our lives. It helps us stay balanced in times of turmoil and keeps us hydrated in the desert of despair. Love softens our hearts, opens our minds, and fuels our growth. It is the nutrient that binds us all, that makes us human, and that enables us to connect on a profound, spiritual level.

The micro elements of our spiritual growth come from our everyday experiences. The joy of success, the pain of failure, the peace of solitude, the warmth of companionship - these experiences shape our character, influence our beliefs and fuel our growth. They are the iron, the zinc, the copper, the molybdenum of our spiritual lives.

Education is a vital nutrient, a force that propels us toward growth. Every lesson learned, and every piece of knowledge gained strengthens our roots and prepares us for the journey ahead. Education shapes our minds, influences our perspective, and equips us with the tools to navigate life's challenges. It is an indispensable element of our spiritual growth, a nutrient we must actively seek and absorb.

Perseverance is the nutrient that strengthens our resolve, making us resilient in the face of adversity. It fortifies our spirit, fuels our growth, and keeps us grounded in our journey. Perseverance is the force that pushes us to keep going, to keep growing, even when the journey becomes challenging. It is the nutrient that prepares us for our divine transplant.

In our lives, we absorb these nutrients from our interactions, experiences, and lessons learned. They nourish our spirit, fuel our growth, and shape our character. They are the essential ingredients of our spiritual journey, the nutrients that prepare us for our divine transplant.

These are the nutrients of our spiritual growth. Like a seed drawing nutrients from the soil, we draw from our experiences, absorb these nutrients, and grow. This is the journey of our spiritual growth, the journey toward our divine transplant. It is not a journey we walk alone. It is a journey guided by divine power, a journey that prepares us for a future beyond our current soil.

Patience can be compared to the soil's organic matter. It facilitates the absorption of other nutrients, making them more readily available to the seed. Patience provides us with the capacity to endure, and to wait for our time of growth and transformation. It teaches us that divine timing is not our own and that every season has its purpose. Patience is the understanding that our divine transplant will come, but it will come in its own time.

Understanding is another critical nutrient in our spiritual lives, similar to the soil's pH. It moderates our internal environment and helps us strike a balance. Understanding enables us to accept and appreciate the diversity of experiences, perspectives, and beliefs that make up our world. It helps us to empathize, to relate, and to see things from different angles. Understanding reminds us that our path is not the only one and that every person's journey is unique.

Next comes courage, the nutrient that emboldens us to face adversity head-on and to stand firm in the face of fear. Courage is the nutrient that pushes us to step out of our comfort zones, take risks, and dare to dream. It empowers us to face our challenges and grow from them. It is courage that will lead us to our divine transplant, giving us the strength to leave our familiar soil behind.

Gratitude is the nutrient that makes what we have

enough and amplifies the blessings of life. It shifts our focus from what's missing to what's present, and from what's wrong to what's right. It invites joy into our lives and contentment into our hearts. Gratitude is the nutrient that enables us to appreciate the journey, the growth, and the preparation for our divine transplant.

Humility is the nutrient that checks our growth and reminds us of our roots. Humility grounds us and helps us remember where we came from. It is the nutrient that allows us to grow without losing sight of our beginnings and without forgetting our soil.

As we absorb these spiritual nutrients, we grow, mature, and prepare for our divine transplant. Like a seed in the soil, we draw from our experiences, our relationships, and our challenges. We extract the nutrients we need, the lessons we learn, and the growth we experience.

Through the nutrients of faith, hope, love, joy, pain, solitude, companionship, education, perseverance, patience, understanding, courage, gratitude, and humility, we grow. They nourish our spirit, prepare us for the journey ahead, and lead us toward our divine transplant. This is our journey of spiritual growth, our journey towards a future beyond our current soil.

4

PRUNING FOR PROSPERITY

*T*here lies a unique beauty in the analogy of a growing plant and a human life, a beauty that is revealed through the process of pruning. Frequently linked with loss, this process inherently involves discomfort. To fully comprehend it, it is essential to delve into the core of a gardener's work.

The gardener, with unwavering commitment, tends to the plants. Regular watering, ensuring optimal sunlight, and providing essential nutrients all form part of a gardener's routine. So is pruning. This might seem counterintuitive. Why would a gardener remove parts of a plant that they've been carefully nurturing?

Pruning isn't simply an act of removal. It is, fundamentally, an act of giving - a gift of health, strength, and abundance. Pruning eliminates the plant's dead or overgrown branches that could be draining its resources. In doing so, it redirects the plant's energy towards new growth, enabling it to thrive and bear more fruit.

In the divine realm, God takes on the role of the diligent gardener. God cares for us, nourishes us, and when the time is right, prunes us. This act might seem harsh and inexplicable from our viewpoint, yet it aligns with God's perspective of greater growth and prosperity.

One might question, how does God prune us? The answer lies in the diverse experiences of our lives. God prunes us through losses, disappointments, and closed doors. These events, though painful, serve a purpose far greater than immediate comfort. They remove elements that may hold us back, paving the way for fresh opportunities and spiritual growth.

Such pruning often thrusts us into discomfort, even grief. The feeling of loss is tangible, the pain palpable. Yet, these experiences foster resilience. They enable us to endure future storms, and to stand firm in the face of adversity. We grow stronger, more resilient. In the grand design of God's garden, these experiences enhance our ability to thrive in the new soil to which we'll eventually be transplanted.

Through the lens of faith, pruning is not punishment. It's preparation. When God prunes, it signals an impending season of growth. It tells us that we are being prepared for a future that holds more than the present. The process may be uncomfortable, even excruciating. Yet, the end product is a person more robust, more capable, and more aligned with God's purpose.

Pruning fosters faith. Faith in the wisdom of the Gardener. Faith that every cut, every loss, contributes to our greater good. It provides a perspective of trust, a perspective that understands that what seems an ending may indeed be a preparation for a new beginning.

Pruning is a divine process. It is an integral part of our spiritual journey, a journey that steers us toward prosperity. Pruning helps us shed unnecessary burdens, grow in resilience, and bloom into our best selves. Remember, it is through the cuts of pruning that the light enters, nurturing the soul within. As we navigate the chapters of life, let's embrace pruning and remember, it is but a divine transition leading us towards the fulfillment of God's greater plan.

Moving forward, it becomes essential to understand that just as every plant reacts differently to pruning, every individual responds differently to God's pruning in their life. What might appear as a setback to one person could be a setup for a greater comeback in God's grand plan.

Pruning also instills patience in us. It teaches us to understand the cyclical nature of growth - that we must retract before we expand, fall before we rise, and let go before we can embrace what's to come. Patience becomes our virtue as we learn to trust the timing of our life and God's plan for us.

Moreover, pruning strengthens our character. Just as a pruned plant develops a sturdier trunk and stronger roots, we too, through our experiences of loss and renewal, develop a firmer foundation of values and an unshaken spirit. This enhanced resilience and character strength help us thrive when we're transplanted to new soil, allowing us to flourish in ways we never thought possible.

At times, it's not just about removing what is unnecessary, but also about making room for what's necessary. A plant cannot grow if it's crowded with dead leaves and overgrown branches, and similarly, our growth is stunted when we hold onto past hurts, failures, and fears. Pruning helps clear the clutter, making space for fresh perspectives, new relationships, and transformative experiences.

And then, there's hope. It's the hope that post-pruning, post-suffering, we will thrive. That the losses and pain will eventually lead to a better, brighter future. This hope gives us the strength to persevere through the darkest times and to stay faithful even when we can't see the light at the end of the tunnel.

Lastly, it's vital to acknowledge that pruning is a continuous process. Just as a gardener prunes a plant season after season, God's pruning in our lives occurs in different phases and at different times. But with each successive pruning, we become more resilient, more grounded in our faith, and more open to receiving God's blessings.

Pruning is not a phase; it's a process, a divine journey that we all must undertake. It's a journey of transformation and growth that prepares us for the divine transplant. Embrace the pruning, embrace the growth, and trust the Gardener. For in the masterful hands of the Gardener, we are not being broken; we are being made.

Thus, as we experience divine pruning, we must remember that the Gardener knows best. It is a part of God's grand design for us. It might hurt, and it might seem confusing, but it is necessary. It prepares us for our divine transplant and ensures that when we are moved, we are ready to grow, thrive, and bloom like never before. After all, the true beauty of a plant is revealed not when it's pruned but when it blossoms post-pruning. Similarly, our true potential is often realized after we've been pruned after we've overcome, and we emerge stronger and wiser.

5

SEASONS OF GROWTH AND DORMANCY

*F*rom the smallest seed to the tallest tree, every plant undergoes a cyclical rhythm of growth and rest, an ebb and flow dictated by the changing seasons. Similarly, we, as individuals on a divine journey, experience our unique rhythm of active periods and quieter times. This rhythm is not an accident; it's an integral part of our spiritual development and a manifestation to God's profound wisdom.

Reflect on the season of spring, a period often associated with renewal and awakening. As new life emerges from the earth, we too can use this season as an opportunity for personal growth and rejuvenation. It's a time to let go of old habits and patterns that no longer serve us and to welcome new beginnings with hope and optimism. By aligning ourselves with our natural rhythm and the changing seasons, we can enhance our connection to the divine and live more authentically in accordance with our true purpose. These new beginnings often follow a period of hardship or loss, providing a refreshing change and a promise of growth. Spring is a season of planting, a time to sow seeds for the future, fostering faith that these seeds will eventually mature into sturdy trees.

Yet, every plant also understands the necessity of summer. A time of warmth and light, summer is a season for growth and maturation. For us, it is a period of progress and productivity, a time to nurture the seeds sown in the spring and encourage their growth. It is during this season that we often see our efforts bear fruit. Our actions, words, and choices during this time significantly impact the shape and size of our harvest.

Then comes the autumn, a season of harvest, a time of reaping what has been sown. In our lives, autumn is the time when we start to see the results of our actions. It is a season of reflection, allowing us to take stock of what we've achieved and where we've grown. It is also a time for gratitude, a chance to thank God for the harvest and the growth that we've experienced.

Yet, it is the winter, the season of dormancy and rest, that often perplexes us most. For a plant, winter is not a time of death but a crucial period of rest and rejuvenation. Similarly, in our spiritual journey, periods of silence, stillness, or apparent inactivity are not indicators of stagnation. They are times for renewal, moments when God is working beneath the surface to prepare us for the new growth that will come with spring.

Understanding these spiritual seasons brings clarity to our journey and purpose to our experiences. Spring teaches us to hope, summer teaches us diligence, autumn teaches us gratitude, and winter teaches us faith. Each season, with its unique lessons, contributes to our overall growth, preparing us for our divine transplant.

These seasons also remind us of God's provision and timing. Just as a gardener knows when to plant, prune, and harvest, God knows the perfect time for every event in our lives. Trusting in God's timing allows us to remain patient during winter and productive during summer. It helps us to appreciate the blossoming of spring and the abundance of autumn.

Remember, these seasons don't always follow a linear pattern. We may experience multiple seasons in a single year, or a single season may span several years. The duration and sequence of these seasons are unique to each of us, reflecting the bespoke nature of God's plan for our lives.

At times, we may find ourselves longing for the productivity of summer during the stillness of winter, or yearning for the freshness of spring during the reflection of autumn. But every season, be it one of growth or dormancy, action or stillness, is crucial for our development. Each is a testament to God's wisdom, a part of our divine journey leading us toward our transplant.

As we navigate our seasons of growth and dormancy, it is essential to embrace each moment, knowing that just as the earth needs all four seasons, we need every season of our spiritual journey. They shape us into who we are and prepare us for what's to come. It is during times of dormancy that we can reflect on our experiences and gain new insights, while the seasons of growth challenge us to push beyond our limits and reach new heights. Embracing these seasons with an open heart and mind allows us to fully appreciate the journey and become the best version of ourselves.

6

WEATHERING STORMS AND DROUGHT

*I*n the natural world, a plant's life is not just cycles of seasons. It is also a series of unpredictable weather events - storms, droughts, floods, and heat waves. These events challenge the plant, pushing it to the brink of its survival. Yet, they also serve to strengthen it, fostering resilience and adaptability that allow it to thrive.

Our spiritual journey is no different. We too face storms and droughts in our lives - times of intense struggle, loss, uncertainty, and hardship. These challenging times can shake our faith, making us question our path and our purpose. However, they also provide an opportunity for growth, a chance to deepen our faith, and foster resilience.

Storms symbolize periods of turbulence and upheaval in our lives. They represent the challenges we didn't foresee, the trials we didn't plan for. In the face of a storm, we may feel overwhelmed, helpless, or even scared. Yet, these very storms, with their fierce winds and torrential rains, have the power to strengthen us.

When a storm strikes a tree, it forces the tree to strengthen its roots to withstand the gusty winds. Similarly, the storms in our lives compel us to dig deeper, to root ourselves firmly in our faith, values, and inner strength. They test our resilience, molding us into individuals capable of withstanding future storms.

Droughts, on the other hand, represent periods of lack, deprivation, or loss. They are times when resources seem scarce, and hope seems faint. Yet, just as plants adapt to survive in drought conditions, we too can adapt and thrive during our spiritual droughts.

During a drought, a plant learns to conserve its resources, to use them judiciously. In the same way, during periods of lack or loss, we learn the art of conservation, the value of gratitude for what we have, and the importance of hope. We also discover our ability to survive and thrive, even when circumstances are less than ideal.

Yet, how do we weather these storms and droughts? The answer lies in faith. Just as a plant doesn't question the storm or the drought but adapts to survive, we too need to adapt and hold onto our faith. We must trust that just as God guides us through seasons of growth and dormancy, God will guide us through our storms and droughts.

Faith provides us with the strength to stand tall during the storm, and to remain hopeful during the drought. It assures us that these trials are not punishments but opportunities for growth, integral parts of our divine journey. Faith reminds us that even the fiercest storm eventually passes, and even the longest drought eventually ends.

Weathering storms and droughts are not just about survival. It is about growth and transformation. It is about learning to stand firm in our faith, even when the winds of life are blowing fiercely. It is about finding hope in the midst of scarcity, about discovering our reservoirs of strength, resilience, and adaptability.

As we weather our storms and droughts, let's remember

that they are temporary. They may shake us, but they cannot break us. They may challenge us, but they cannot defeat us. Instead, they equip us, preparing us for the divine transplant. They provide us with the strength, resilience, and faith needed to thrive in the new soil where we are destined to bloom.

Reflecting on my personal journey, the concept of resilience takes on profound significance. The year was 2020, a time when a global pandemic held the world in its unforgiving grip. I was employed with a cruise line, a job that provided not just a steady income, but also immense personal satisfaction. Yet, as the pandemic's effects spread, halting cruise operations worldwide, I found myself suddenly jobless. The steady life I was accustomed to came to a standstill.

Unemployment, a word I had never thought would define my life, became my reality. The days turned into weeks, and the weeks into months. Six grueling months of joblessness made life a struggle. Bills piled up, my pantry gradually emptied, and hope seemed elusive. It felt like a relentless drought, a drought that was drying up not just my resources, but my spirit as well.

Just when despair was about to consume me, a flicker of an idea sparked within me. The world was changing, moving towards a digital realm. I could either lament the loss of the old world or adapt and embrace the new one. I chose the latter. I enrolled in online courses, learning new skills, and equipping myself for the evolving digital workforce. I pivoted from the conventional to the remote, from in-person offices to the virtual workspace.

My first job offer post-pandemic came at $6 per hour. Not a lucrative wage, yet it was a beacon of hope in the bleakness. From this point, I witnessed a transformation, both in my professional life and within myself. My wage started growing, from \$6 to \$12, from \$12 to \$18, and beyond.

Along this journey, I learned not just to survive but also to thrive. My skills, once confined to the cruise line industry, expanded to encompass a broader, more diverse skillset. As I climbed out of the financial pit, I reached out to others, sharing my knowledge, teaching them how to freelance, how to navigate this new digital world.

The storm of the pandemic and the drought of unemployment, while challenging, catalyzed a period of immense growth. It made me resilient, adaptable, and resourceful. It transformed my professional life, but more importantly, it enriched my personal growth and spiritual journey.

My experience illustrates how storms and droughts in our lives, however difficult, are not mere periods of hardship. They are opportunities, gateways to personal growth and spiritual enlightenment. They foster resilience, stir innovation, and lead us to find new paths.

What seemed like a crushing storm led me to a path of continual growth and enabled me to assist others in their journeys. This personal storm was not just about weathering, it was about learning, growing, and evolving. It was a testament to faith, resilience, and adaptability. It was proof to God's divine plan, a plan that prepared me for a new season, a divine transplant.

My journey underscores that hardships and trials, the storms and droughts of our lives, are chapters in our divine journey. They shape us, mold us, and prepare us for the future that God has planned for us. They equip us with the strength, resilience, and faith needed to thrive in the new soil where we are destined to bloom.

7

THE GRAFTING PROCESS

*I*n the intricate world of botany, there is a remarkable procedure known as grafting. This is not merely an act but rather a methodical process, combining two plants in such a way that they grow together, forming a singular entity. The strength and resilience of one intertwine with the vibrant characteristics of the other, resulting in a plant that boasts attributes of both parents. As in horticulture, so too in our spiritual lives, we are called to experience this profound fusion with the Divine.

Grafting may seem like an odd notion to the untrained eye, but in essence, it is a deliberate act of unity. It symbolizes the profound connection that we can cultivate with God. This process isn't always straightforward, it requires patience, trust, and a deep understanding that the benefits of such a union surpass any temporary discomfort or fear.

In the hands of an experienced gardener, two key components are carefully selected for grafting: the rootstock and the scion. The rootstock is that part of the plant which remains steadfastly in the earth. This is selected for its fortitude, its ability to thrive in harsh environments, and its tenacious resilience. The scion, on the other hand, is a bud or twig meant for grafting onto the rootstock. It is chosen not for its present state but for its future promise – its potential to yield a bounty of fruit and a proliferation of blossoms.

So it is with us and God, we represent the scions. Our hearts are repositories of untapped potential and dreams that are yet to manifest.God symbolizes the rootstock, embodying unfathomable strength, wisdom, and an enduring love that can withstand the severest storms.

Grafting asks for a kind of surrender. Like the scion that must leave its solitary life to join with the rootstock, it involves giving up control and trusting in the process. It's about accepting change and being open to transformation.

Much like the grafting process, intertwining our lives with God requires us to yield control. We must surrender to His will, entrust our dreams and fears to Him, and believe in His love. This surrender doesn't make us weak, it makes us strong, resilient and allows us to bloom in ways we never thought possible.

As the scion becomes part of the rootstock, the grafting wound begins to heal. A bridge of new cells forms across the wound, connecting the scion and the rootstock. This connection, known as the callus, is the bond that holds the two together.

In our connection with God, there are times when we feel wounded, unsure, and vulnerable. The healing from this vulnerability forms a callus, a strengthened bond with God. It's in these moments of deep connection that we find ourselves grafted into Him, growing stronger, more resilient, and more rooted in our faith.

The process of grafting, once complete, offers the promise of extraordinary growth. A simple twig, once vulnerable and susceptible, now stands tall, strengthened by its union with the rootstock. Its potential for bearing fruit multiplies, and it thrives, undeterred by the winds that once threatened to break it.

As we surrender ourselves and intertwine our lives with God, we tap into this extraordinary potential. Our lives become enriched, our capacities expand, and we bear the fruits of love, peace, patience, kindness, goodness, faithfulness, gentleness, and self-control. These fruits are not just for our consumption but are meant to nourish others, spreading the love of God far and wide.

In the world of botany, the process of grafting may take a season, perhaps two. But the rewards of the process, the abundance it brings, make it a worthwhile endeavor. In our lives, the grafting process may take time, and it may require patience and faith, but the fruits it bears, and the strength it bestows, make it a journey worth undertaking.

The grafting process generally begins amid life's thorny patches. One such instance occurred in my personal path when I found myself living with a foster family. It was not an easy time; the family had hyper-religious views, practiced extreme religious practices, and did not accept me for who I was: a strong-willed and independent individual. As a stranger in a strange land, I felt the agony of emotional abuse and discrimination from them for not fitting in. This situation appeared to be intolerable, an experience that I felt I did not deserve.

However, through this experience, I learned the value of perseverance and resilience, and how to adapt to challenging situations. This taught me that the grafting process can lead to personal growth and development, even in the most difficult circumstances.

So, how does this tie into grafting, you might wonder. Much like the scion separated from its original plant and placed onto a new rootstock, I felt detached from my former life. This feeling of displacement, of not belonging, was as confusing as it was painful. It felt like being buried in the soil of discomfort and prejudice.

Yet, when I consider the parable of the wheat and the tares in the book of Matthew, I find a profound connection with my experience. The parable speaks of a field where wheat and weeds grow together. The owner of the field instructs his servants to let the wheat and weeds grow together until harvest time. At harvest, the wheat is gathered into the barn, while the weeds are bundled up and burned.

It's tempting to believe that our lives should only have the "wheat," the good things, and the comfortable situations. But God, in His infinite wisdom, allows the "wheat" and "tares" to grow together. It's in this mix of the good and the challenging that our true growth occurs.

My time with the foster family, however challenging, was an important part of my life's grafting process. The harsh circumstances acted like the gardener's knife in the grafting process, cutting away from my comfort zone and creating a wound. But it was a necessary wound, for it prepared me for the union that was to follow.

This grueling experience caused me to turn to God in ways I had never done before. It was a time of surrender, of giving up control and relying on God's strength to get through it. Throughout this process, I found myself grafting onto Him, leaning into His strength and wisdom in the midst of adversity. Like the grafting callus that strengthens the relationship between the scion and rootstock, my faith and trust in Him grew.

Today, I recognize that the "tares" of my past served a purpose in my spiritual growth. Just as the gardener allows the scion and rootstock to experience the harsh cut of the knife, God allowed me to experience difficult situations to prepare me for the fruitful life He planned for me. Just as the grafting process results in a stronger, more resilient plant, my experiences resulted in a stronger, more resilient faith.

In hindsight, this difficult chapter of my life was not a punishment, but a grafting into something much bigger than myself. It was my training ground, a transformative phase where I became intimately connected with God. And from this connection, I emerged stronger, more resilient, and prepared to face the winds of life, just like the grafted scion standing tall with the rootstock.

Indeed, the concept of divine grafting brings a fresh perspective to the adversities we face in life. Even when surrounded by "tares," or difficult circumstances, there is a divine purpose at work, a grafting process in progress. So let the "wheat" and "tares" grow together, for each has a role to play in our spiritual growth.

8

PUSH FORWARD YOUR
TRANSPLANT IS NEAR

*E*ach season ushers in change, evolution, and progress. Within the life cycle of a plant, there comes a moment when its roots outgrow the confines of the pot it has been nurtured in. The plant then needs to be transplanted into a larger pot or directly into the ground.

A gardener discerns the need for a transplant through various signs. The plant's growth may slow, its roots might begin to circle the bottom of the pot or start poking out of the drainage holes, or perhaps the plant begins to wilt despite receiving proper care. These signs indicate the plant's readiness for a transplant, a change of environment that fosters further growth.

Life mirrors this process in a multitude of ways. Spiritual stagnation, recurring obstacles, or continual discomfort can often be indications of an impending divine transplant. These signs can be tough to interpret and can lead to discomfort and anxiety. However, remember that these signals suggest an imminent shift, a preparation for something new and expansive.

Reflect on a time when life seemed to stand still when the

joy and growth that were once present seemed to vanish. This sensation of stagnation can be disconcerting, reminiscent of the stunted growth of a plant in need of a transplant. It might be hard to comprehend why the growth and progress once enjoyed seem to have abruptly halted. Yet, this is a signal, a hint that a season of expansion is near, that a divine transplant is on the horizon.

Discomfort, too, serves as an indicator. Much like the plant roots pushing against the confines of the pot, our souls often strain against the limitations of our comfort zones. These moments of discomfort are not designed to cause distress, but to signal that a transplant is imminent.

Recurrent obstacles can also be signposts for an upcoming divine transplant. Just like the gardener who notices the roots encircling the bottom of the pot, life may present us with circular obstacles – repetitive challenges that seem never-ending. These obstacles are not roadblocks but signposts, pointing towards the need for a divine transplant.

However, recognizing these signs is just the first step. The subsequent action following this awareness is crucial. A good gardener, upon noticing these signs, prepares for the transplant. They select a larger pot, prepare fresh soil, and take measures to minimize damage to the plant during the transplant.

In our lives, recognizing the signs of a divine transplant should lead to preparation. This preparation might involve abandoning old habits, cultivating new ones, seeking wisdom in prayer and scripture, and maintaining an openness to change. It's about making space for new growth, releasing the old, and welcoming the new with open arms and an open heart.

A plant's transplant does not occur without care. The gardener handles the plant delicately, ensuring the roots remain unharmed, and provides ample water and sunlight post-transplant. Similarly, a divine transplant occurs with infinite love and care. God, the divine gardener, handles each soul with gentleness, ensuring minimal harm and offering abundant love and care throughout the process.

Recognizing the signs of a divine transplant is not always straightforward. It requires spiritual discernment, a profound connection with God, and a willingness to move beyond the familiar. However, with each sign, whether it's spiritual stagnation, recurrent obstacles, or persistent discomfort, remember that these are precursors to a season of growth.

So take heart when you see these signs. Do not perceive them as hindrances but as signals that a divine transplant is imminent. Prepare for the shift, make room for new growth, and trust the process.

Reflecting back on my younger years, I recall a moment of deep pain and despair. I was at my lowest, feeling as if I were trapped in a never-ending cycle of difficulties. Amid this turmoil, I received this revelation of the divine transplant, which has completely changed my perspective from that point forward.

During that dark period, I found myself seeking solace and guidance in prayer more fervently than ever before. I distinctly remember one night, when in the midst of pouring out my heart to God, I was desperately searching for some understanding, for some reassurance that my turmoil was temporary. It was then that I received a message, one which at the time, I struggled to fully comprehend.

In the tranquility that followed my fervent prayer, I felt a quiet yet distinct impression in my heart. The message was clear: "Be still, I am preparing you for a transplant, a divine transplant." At that time, as a teenager grappling with life's hardships, the concept of a divine transplant seemed foreign, even puzzling.

In the years that ensued, that message served as a beacon of hope for me, a source of comfort in trying times. The concept of a divine transplant began to resonate, particularly when I reflected on experiences that had initially seemed unbearable.

The seasons of stagnation, the recurring obstacles, the persistent discomfort - all these were signs that a divine transplant was imminent. The challenges I faced were similar to a plant outgrowing its pot, its roots yearning for more room, longing for the freedom to expand and grow.

The revelation about the divine transplant was not an immediate solution to the problems I was facing. Rather, it was a promise of future transformation, a reassurance that the trials and tribulations were priming me for a significant shift.

With this insight, I began to approach my struggles from a different angle. I started viewing them as preparations for my transplant, rather than mere suffering. I started to understand that I was in a season of being uprooted from familiar territory and being readied for a relocation to a place where I could flourish.

My divine transplant did not occur overnight, nor was it a straightforward process. But in retrospect, every sign, every challenge, was a step towards this transplant. Today, I stand firm in the knowledge that the signs I experienced were part of a bigger plan, a divine blueprint that facilitated personal growth and spiritual deepening.

Looking back, I understand that the revelation I received as a teenager was a seed planted by God, one that would take years to sprout, grow, and eventually bear fruit. This understanding didn't exempt me from life's difficulties, but it provided a lens through which I could view these experiences as growth opportunities rather than mere suffering.

So, when you find yourself in the midst of hardships,

feeling as if the world is against you, remember that you could be in preparation for a divine transplant. Learn to recognize the signs, perceive the signals of an upcoming shift, and take heart. For even in the most challenging circumstances, there is a promise of growth, of a transplant leading to a more abundant life.

9

RECOGNIZING THE SIGNS OF A DIVINE TRANSPLANT

*L*earning to recognize the signs of an impending divine transplant is a pivotal part of one's spiritual journey. Just as a gardener becomes adept at reading the signals given by a plant in need of a larger environment, we too can cultivate an awareness of the signs that indicate our readiness for a divine transplant.

One such sign could be a sense of spiritual stagnation. If you find yourself in a place where spiritual growth seems stunted, where your prayers seem unanswered, or your relationship with God feels distant, it might be a sign that a divine transplant is imminent. This sense of stagnation is akin to the slowed growth of a plant ready for transplanting. It's a call to prepare for a move into a more expansive spiritual environment.

A second sign could be the recurrence of certain challenges or obstacles. If you find yourself repeatedly confronted with the same difficulties, as if trapped in a cycle, it might be a signal that you're ready for a divine transplant. Much like the plant whose roots circle the bottom of the pot, encountering the same obstacle over and over again, your recurring challenges may be nudging you towards a larger space for growth.

A third sign could be the experience of discomfort. Discomfort often acts as a potent catalyst for change. If you find yourself feeling increasingly uncomfortable in your current circumstances, it may be a sign of an impending divine transplant. This is akin to the plant whose roots have outgrown its pot, causing it to wilt despite proper care. The discomfort you're experiencing might be nudging you to prepare for a shift, to ready yourself for an environment that will allow for expanded growth.

A fourth sign might be the feeling of being out of sync with your surroundings. Just as a plant starts showing signs of stress when it outgrows its pot, you might start feeling as though you no longer fit into your environment, as if you're growing in a direction that your current circumstances don't support. This feeling of being out of place could be a signal that you're ready for a divine transplant.

These signs - spiritual stagnation, recurrent obstacles, persistent discomfort, and feeling out of sync - are not definitive. They are merely signals, indications, whispers from the Divine, pointing toward the impending transplant. They may vary in intensity and duration, and they may manifest differently for each individual.

However, once you learn to recognize these signs, you are better equipped for the upcoming divine transplant. You can take the necessary steps to prepare yourself - letting go of old habits, fostering new ones, seeking wisdom in prayer and scripture, and being open to change.

Remember, these signs are not indicators of failure or punishment, but signals of an imminent shift, a divine transplant. Like the plant ready to be moved to a larger pot, these signs indicate your readiness to step into a broader spiritual environment, one where you can flourish and grow more abundantly. Embrace the signs, prepare for the shift, and trust the process, knowing that the Divine Gardener is at work, preparing you for your divine transplant.

10

THE DIVINE TRANSPLANT

*I*n the realm of horticulture, a transplant is an operation that moves a plant from one location to another, enabling it to grow more vigorously, bloom more beautifully, or bear more fruit. The same holds true for a divine transplant - a relocation orchestrated by the Divine to provide fertile ground for our spiritual growth.

The divine transplant is more than just a mere shift; it's a profound transformation, a deep-seated change that offers the promise of renewal, growth, and increased spiritual fruitfulness. It's the journey of moving from the familiar soil that once nurtured us but now stifles our growth to the new soil that promises abundance and expansion.

Our spiritual journey is sprinkled with divine transplants. These turning points redefine our relationship with God, reshape our understanding of the Divine, and renew our spiritual growth. They come in different forms and at different times, tailored to our unique spiritual needs and growth trajectory.

Divine transplants are not always smooth. Like a plant being uprooted and replanted, they may involve an uncomfortable transition. However, they are necessary for our spiritual development. Through these divine transplants, we're given the opportunity to dig deeper into the richness of our relationship with God, to root ourselves in faith and spirituality, and to grow into our full spiritual potential.

God, our Divine Gardener, handles each divine transplant with infinite care and wisdom. The process, although it may involve a degree of discomfort, is designed to minimize shock and maximize growth. Just as the gardener carefully removes the plant from its old pot, loosens the root ball, and places it in new soil, God gently guides us through each divine transplant, ensuring that we are nurtured and supported throughout the process.

Each divine transplant demonstrates God's loving care and commitment to our spiritual growth. It's a sign of God's trust in our ability to adapt, grow, and flourish in new spiritual environments. It's a reminder that God has a plan for us, a divine blueprint designed for our spiritual prosperity.

Divine transplants challenge us, test our faith, and take us out of our comfort zones. However, they also provide us with unparalleled opportunities for growth, renewal, and deepening our relationship with God. They are the seasons in our lives when we are pruned, uprooted, and replanted in more fertile soil where we can grow more abundantly.

So, embrace the divine transplant. Welcome the discomfort, the unfamiliarity, and the uncertainty that comes with it. Recognize it as an opportunity for growth, renewal, and a deeper connection with God. View it as the beginning of a new chapter in your spiritual journey, a chapter filled with promise and potential.

Trust the Divine Gardener. Have faith in the process. Remember that every transplant is guided by infinite wisdom and love. Remember that every discomfort, every challenge, is a stepping stone to growth. And remember that every divine transplant is a step closer to realizing your spiritual potential, blooming more beautifully, and bearing more fruit.

With every divine transplant, you are being moved closer to your divine destiny, guided to a space where your roots can spread, your growth can accelerate, and your spiritual fruits can multiply. With each divine transplant, you are becoming more deeply rooted in God, more firmly planted in faith, and more abundantly fruitful in your spiritual journey.

Reflecting on my personal journey, a recent divine transplant that immediately comes to mind occurred in 2022, a significant shift that took me from my home country of Jamaica to the United States. At the time, I had no inkling that such a move was on the horizon or that I would soon be pursuing my dream of studying for a degree in Law at a college in the United States.

The whisper of the spirit came to me in a moment of seeming stability, just when life was finally taking a turn for the better. Financial hurdles had been overcome, I was engaged in online education, and a well-paying job provided a comfortable livelihood. In my mind, it was a season of rejuvenation, of steady growth.

But, as I learned, the spirit's wisdom transcends human comprehension. The whisper urged me to prepare for a shift, indicating that my current state, though comforting, was merely transient. It signaled that the soil I had been growing in, my Jamaican homeland, could no longer sustain my growth. A divine transplant was imminent.

Within the blink of an eye, my life was upended. A student visa was petitioned, every possession in my apartment was sold, and I bid farewell to the familiar surroundings of my home country. With faith as my guiding light, I embarked on a new chapter in the United States.

The honor of being a first-generation college student in my family, particularly on my mother's side, brings with it a sense of profound achievement. As the first to graduate from high school and advance to tertiary education, I fulfilled my aspiration of being a role model for my younger brother, something I lacked growing up.

The anxiety about transitioning from online to campus education and grappling with the currency disparity between Jamaican dollars and US dollars seemed daunting initially. Yet, as the divine transplant took place, a miraculous revelation unfolded. Upon my arrival, the new soil was already prepared. Opportunities began to spring forth like seeds quickened into life by the warmth of the sun. The journey, which initially seemed intimidating, has been remarkably smooth.

Looking back, the divine transplant unraveled as a shift from a cycle of emotional abuse to a state of genuine happiness. The heavy chains of poverty were broken, replaced with the freedom and potential of wealth. From the ashes of generational curses, I rose, becoming a catalyst for positive change within my family.

The divine transplant, though challenging, has turned into a profound blessing. It was a move not just across geographical boundaries but across emotional and spiritual landscapes as well. It exemplifies the power of faith, the resilience of the human spirit, and the grace of divine guidance. It serves as a reminder that even in moments of stability, we must remain open to the whispers of the spirit, ready to embrace the divine transplants that lead us to broader horizons and deeper growth.

11

THRIVING IN NEW SOIL

*N*ew soil, with its distinct texture and unique properties, can initially seem daunting to any plant, let alone to us humans undergoing a divine transplant. Yet, it's within this unfamiliar terrain that the most profound growth often occurs. The uncertainty that accompanies such unfamiliar environments provides a fertile breeding ground for resilience, adaptability, and spiritual expansion.

Consider this new soil as an invitation to grow beyond previous limitations. It's an opportunity to delve deeper into one's spiritual roots, rise above the surface of familiarity, and extend one's branches into uncharted spiritual territories. This new environment, while initially discomforting, is teeming with potential for personal and spiritual growth.

A divine transplant into new soil is rarely a smooth journey. Like a plant adjusting to its new environment, you may face initial hurdles. There may be moments of doubt, of longing for the familiar, of wrestling with the unknown. Such feelings are natural. They are an inherent part of the adaptation process. Yet, with time, patience, and faith, you will acclimate to the new soil and begin to flourish.

Learning to thrive in new soil is about embracing change and exploring the unfamiliar with a heart full of faith and a mind open to growth. It's about finding the Divine in the unfamiliar, recognizing the spiritual nutrients present in the new soil, and using them to spur your growth.

With every challenge encountered in the new soil, remember, you are growing, evolving, and becoming more resilient. Every struggle is an opportunity for you to deepen your roots in faith, strengthen your relationship with God, and expand your spiritual understanding.

In the new soil, you will discover hidden strengths, uncover latent talents, and experience spiritual growth in ways you could never have imagined. You will learn to navigate unfamiliar terrains, adapt to new environments, and grow more robust with each passing season.

The new soil is where your potential is realized. It's where you flourish, where you bloom, where you bear fruit. It's where you evolve from a seedling into a mature, fruit-bearing tree, deeply rooted in faith and abundantly fruitful in your spiritual journey.

Adapting to and growing in new soil is not merely about surviving; it's about thriving. It's about welcoming the opportunities that come with the unfamiliar, celebrating the growth that follows adversity, and rejoicing in the bountiful spiritual harvest that comes from living and growing in new soil.

So, delve into the richness of your new soil. Explore its depths, embrace its challenges, and celebrate its opportunities. Let your roots grow deep, let your branches reach high, and let your leaves bask in the sunlight of Divine love. Thrive in your new soil, for it is in this very soil that your spiritual journey will bloom into its fullest, most beautiful expression.

As you grow accustomed to the new soil, take a moment to reflect on the path that brought you here, the divine transplant that moved you from familiar grounds to uncharted territories. With every experience, you've become a part of the new environment, absorbing its unique characteristics and contributing your essence to its richness.

Embracing new soil requires a level of surrender. It involves letting go of previous notions and assumptions and making room for fresh perspectives and experiences. Surrender, in this context, isn't about giving up; rather, it's about yielding to the divine wisdom that oversees your spiritual journey. It's about trusting the process, recognizing that the divine transplant was not an arbitrary event, but a significant milestone in your life's spiritual trajectory.

In the new soil, you'll find unique experiences that contribute to your spiritual growth. Like a plant responding to the changing seasons, you'll learn to navigate various phases of life. Every experience is an invitation to grow, to deepen your relationship with the divine, and to actualize your potential.

Your spiritual journey in the new soil is not a solo endeavor. Just as plants in an ecosystem are interconnected, your journey is intertwined with those around you. The connections you form, the relationships you nurture, the communities you become a part of - these are integral aspects of your growth in the new soil. They offer invaluable opportunities to learn, share, and grow.

As you adapt to your new environment, remember that the process doesn't have to be perfect. Growth, in nature and in our spiritual journeys, is often messy, non-linear, and filled with uncertainties. The divine transplant didn't promise an easy journey, but it assured growth, resilience, and ultimately, a bountiful harvest.

In the broader scope of life, divine transplants are an integral part of our spiritual evolution. The new soil is your new beginning, an opportunity to redefine your relationship with the divine, explore your spiritual capabilities, and grow into the best version of yourself. In this soil, you're not merely surviving; you're thriving, and becoming an embodiment of divine grace.

So, as you journey through this new soil, let it mold you, shape you, and transform you. Embrace the challenges, celebrate the triumphs, and remain open to the profound lessons that come with every experience. The divine transplant was not the end of your journey, but a new beginning, a leap into a vibrant spiritual adventure. Here in this soil, the divine story continues, and you are its central character, beautifully thriving and continuously evolving.

12

GROWING INTO YOUR POTENTIAL

*a*n intriguing aspect of the divine transplant lies in the potential it unlocks. Just like a seed that holds the blueprint for a mighty tree, we all harbor immense potential within us, waiting for the right conditions to unfold. It's in the new soil, this uncharted terrain, where the realization of this potential takes place.

Consider this potential as the unique combination of abilities, talents, strengths, and divine gifts that are distinctively yours. It's the divine DNA, the spiritual blueprint that guides your growth and transformation. As you settle into the new soil, you embark on a journey of unfolding this potential, of growing into the divine plan meant for you.

Growing into your potential is about nurturing your inherent gifts, cultivating your strengths, and expanding your capabilities. It's about recognizing the unique traits you bring to this world and using them to contribute positively to your surroundings. It's about allowing the divine plan to unfold gracefully, leading to the blossoming of your full spiritual self.

Every experience in the new soil contributes to this

process. Each challenge faced, every victory achieved, and all the lessons learned, they're all crucial elements nurturing your growth. Like a sculptor chipping away at a block of marble to reveal the masterpiece within, these experiences slowly unveil the magnitude of your potential.

The journey of growing into your potential is unique to each individual. It's not about comparing your growth with others, but about aligning yourself with the divine plan for your life. It's about acknowledging your unique rhythm of growth and celebrating the uniqueness of your journey.

As you continue to grow, you will notice shifts in your perspectives, expansions in your understanding, and deepening of your spiritual wisdom. These are signs that you're not only growing but thriving, becoming the best version of yourself. They indicate that you're stepping into your potential, becoming the person you were divinely designed to be.

Remember, the journey to realizing your potential is not a race, but a graceful dance of growth. There's no set timeline or pre-defined path. It's a personal journey, guided by divine wisdom, fueled by faith, and marked by personal and spiritual growth.

The divine transplant, the shift to the new soil, was the beginning of this journey. It set the stage for your potential to be unveiled, for your unique gifts to be nurtured and for your spiritual growth to be realized. With every passing moment in this new soil, you're growing into your potential, blooming into your spiritual self, and becoming a living manifestation of grace.

So, as you navigate through this new soil, take a moment to appreciate your growth. Celebrate the progress made, the milestones achieved, and the potential realized. Remember, the journey of growing into your potential is a divine dance of transformation, a sacred process of becoming, a witness to the power of divine transplant. It's your unique journey of transformation, a journey into the fullest, most authentic expression of your divine self.

As you journey deeper into your potential, you might experience moments of doubt, questioning whether you're capable of realizing the divine plan. These moments, while uncomfortable, are integral to your journey. They prompt introspection, foster resilience, and nudge you to explore your inner depth.

Embracing your potential isn't about perfection; it's about growth and progression. It's about taking incremental steps toward the divine blueprint etched within your spirit. Each step, no matter how small, brings you closer to your full potential.

Navigating this path, remember to extend kindness and compassion to yourself. The journey to realizing your potential is strewn with challenges and triumphs, setbacks and leaps, doubts and affirmations. Treat these experiences as essential components of your growth, reminders of your human resilience and divine connection.

Growing into your potential also requires patience. Just as a seed takes time to germinate, grow, and bear fruit, your potential unfolds over time. Trust the divine timing. Allow your potential to blossom at its own pace. Your journey is not defined by how quickly you reach your destination, but by the growth and transformation that occur along the way.

As you continue your journey in the new soil, you'll notice a profound change within yourself. You'll see your strengths magnifying, your talents flourishing, and your spiritual connection deepening. You'll observe yourself adapting to the new environment, thriving amidst challenges, and progressively aligning with the divine purpose.

Growing into your potential shows your resilience and adaptability. It's a celebration of the divine plan that unfolds in your life, an affirmation of the divine wisdom that guides your path. It's an acknowledgment of your growth, a recognition of your spiritual evolution.

As your journey continues, let every moment be a reminder of your divine potential. Let every experience strengthen your faith, deepen your understanding, and fortify your commitment to growth. You are a divine creation, growing and thriving in the new soil, progressively embodying your full potential.

Remember, the divine transplant was the catalyst for this journey. It relocated you to the new soil, setting the stage for your growth and transformation. Here, in this new environment, you're not just surviving; you're thriving, growing, and evolving. You're embracing your divine potential, becoming the best version of yourself.

So, keep growing, keep striving, keep evolving. Let your life be a shining example of the power of divine transplant, a celebration of your growth into your fullest potential. In this new soil, you're not just a seed; you're a flourishing plant, continually maturing and becoming a living proof of the transformative influence of grace.

13

THE HARVEST

*A*rriving at the point of harvest is a monumental milestone on the journey of a divine transplant. It symbolizes the fruition of your spiritual evolution, the result of your persistence, resilience, and unyielding faith. It's the visible manifestation of the divine plan that has been unfolding since the initiation of your divine transplant.

The harvest is not merely a culmination of your efforts, it's a celebration of your journey. It's an affirmation of the divine wisdom that guided your path, a testament to your courage in facing the unknown, and a nod to your determination in embracing your potential.

As you stand amidst your harvest, take a moment to look back at your journey. Reflect on the experiences that have led you here, the moments of joy and sorrow, the triumphs and challenges, the growth and transformation. Each experience, each moment, has contributed to the richness of your harvest.

In the context of your divine transplant, the harvest is symbolic. It represents the manifestation of your divine potential, the realization of your spiritual capabilities, and the blossoming of your unique gifts. Your harvest is the physical manifestation of your divine essence, a testament to your spiritual growth.

Your harvest is also a beacon for those on their journey. It serves as a symbol of hope, a testament to the potential of divine transplant. Your harvest illuminates the path for others, offering guidance, encouragement, and inspiration. It shows that despite the challenges, uncertainties, and upheavals, a bountiful harvest awaits at the end of the journey.

As you stand among your harvest, take a moment to feel grateful. Thank the wisdom that guided you, the experiences that made you stronger, the challenges that tested you, and the victories that lifted your spirits. This gratitude can make your joy even more meaningful.

Remember, the harvest isn't the end of your journey. Just like a farmer who gets ready for the next season after a harvest, your path continues beyond this point. This harvest gets you ready for the next part of your spiritual journey, setting the stage for even more growth and change.

As you stand among your harvest, let your heart fill with joy, your spirit shine with thanks, and your mind be full of wisdom. The path of your divine transplant has led you here, to a place of fulfillment, growth, and wisdom.

Right now, you're not just a part of a divine plan. You're living proof of its power. You've gone from seed to harvest, from a young plant to a flourishing one. Your harvest is a sign of this journey, a sign of the power of divine grace.

As you celebrate your harvest, remember the path that led you here. Let it serve as a beacon of hope for others, lighting their way. Your harvest isn't just the end of a journey. It's the start of many more to come.

In the next stage of your spiritual journey, keep nurturing your spirit, seeking divine guidance, and growing stronger and wiser. As you move forward, may you continue to grow, flourish, and inspire.

14

A PRAYER FOR FAITH AND GROWTH AMIDST DIVINE TRANSPLANT

*D*ear Divine Creator, in Your infinite wisdom and grace, I seek guidance and strength as I journey through the process of my divine transplant. Amidst the uncertainties, discomfort, and frustration, help me find the courage to trust in Your plan, to lean into the challenges, and to celebrate the growth that arises from every encounter.

Even when the soil of my life feels foreign and the terrain rough, remind me that this is the fertile ground where seeds of change take root, where transformation begins. During times of discomfort and frustration, help me remember that the most beautiful blooms are often the result of the most rigorous growth process.

I declare that no matter how uncomfortable the process, no matter how trying the situation, I will push forward, anchored by faith, guided by divine wisdom, and fueled by the promise of a bountiful harvest.

Help me recognize that discomfort is but a sign of growth, a testament to my evolving spirit. Grant me the courage to embrace the unknown, to weather the storms, and to stand resilient in the face of adversity. May I see every challenge not as an obstacle, but as an opportunity for growth.

As I push past discomfort and frustration, may I grow in strength, wisdom, and grace. Help me remember that even in moments of doubt, Your hand guides me, Your love surrounds me, and Your light leads the way.

I declare that with every step on this journey, I am not alone. I am guided, protected, and loved. I believe in the power of divine transplant, in the transformative journey from seed to harvest, from discomfort to growth.

I trust in Your timing, in Your plan, in the divine wisdom that orchestrates my divine transplant. As I journey through this process, may I never lose sight of the harvest that awaits me, the bountiful manifestation of Your love and grace.

And so, I declare with unwavering faith - through the discomfort, through the frustration, I will push forward. I will grow. I will transform. And I will celebrate the bountiful harvest of this divine transplant.

In Your holy name, I pray. Amen.

ABOUT THE AUTHOR

Oshane Hines is a dynamic young entrepreneur, spiritual teacher, and spiritual warfare specialist hailing from the vibrant heart of Jamaica. His journey in the business world began with the foundation of HinesPress, a trailblazing digital publishing company designed to empower and inspire authors in the digital age.

Oshane's work encompasses far more than entrepreneurial ventures. A passionate spiritual teacher, he brings an uncommon depth of insight to his teachings. Guided by an innate desire to decode and illuminate spiritual teachings and Biblical scripture, his approach is innovative, resonating with the modern seeker. As a spiritual warfare specialist, Oshane stands on the front lines, equipping individuals with the tools and wisdom they need to navigate and triumph over spiritual battles.

His writing merges the realms of business, spirituality, and personal development in an inspiring, pragmatic style. Oshane's life experiences, coupled with his Jamaican heritage, bring a refreshing perspective to his works, making his voice a beacon for readers seeking to find their path in a complex world.

Dedicated to uplifting others and fostering a deep understanding of spiritual principles, Oshane Hines is a leading voice in the evolution of contemporary spirituality and publishing, boldly shaping the narrative for a new generation of authors and spiritual warriors.

in

www.ingramcontent.com/pod-product-compliance
Lightning Source LLC
Chambersburg PA
CBHW031614040426
42452CB00006B/511